CHARLES DICKENS

A Life from Beginning to End

Copyright © 2018 by Hourly History.

All rights reserved.

Table of Contents

Introduction
Providing for His Family as a Child
Beginnings as an Author
Increasing Fame
The Republic of My Imagination
Ghosts and Growing Troubles
Personal and Public Hardships
Rumors and Infidelity
Return to America and Last Years
Conclusion

Introduction

Charles Dickens established a reputation as a novelist that has carried his work through a century and a half. The titles of many of his works, like *David Copperfield, Nicholas Nickleby,* or *Great Expectations,* are widely recognized; even some of the lines contained in his books, such as *Oliver Twist*'s "Please sir, may I have some more?" or the famed opening lines of *A Tale of Two Cities,* "It was the best of times, it was the worst of times." have become well known. His works have translated well into other mediums as well—most of his works have now been adapted into movies or TV series, just as they were adapted for the stage in his own lifetime. Many people watch one of the over a dozen film renditions of *The Christmas Carol* year after year, even if they've never read one of Dickens' novels.

Still, few know much about Charles Dickens beyond his famous name. His experiences as a boy, particularly the year he spent as a 12-year-old working in a shoe-blacking factory while his father was in debtor's prison, had great influence on his writing. He was always observant, able to create dramatic characters by building on his lifetime of close scrutiny of people. Often people he knew inspired his characters, from his sister's four-year-old crippled son who turned into *A Christmas Carol*'s Tiny Tim, to his first love, Maria Beadnell, whom he would unkindly use as inspiration for the depiction of overweight, drunken Flora Finching in *Little Dorrit*.

Though Dickens could be hot-headed and impulsive, he was concerned about the society he lived in and wanted to bring about change. In this book, you'll meet Charles Dickens, the man who loved theatre, was crossed in love, survived a train wreck, tried to change the way his society viewed and dealt with poverty, and who not only produced novels but also helped raise the genre of the novel itself to popularity.

Chapter One

Providing for His Family as a Child

"No words can express the secret agony of my soul . . . the sense I had of being utterly neglected and hopeless; of the shame I felt in my position . . . My whole nature was penetrated with grief and humiliation."

—Charles Dickens, recalling his work in the blacking factory

In the suburb of Landport, outside Portsmouth, Elizabeth Dickens gave birth to her second child on February 7, 1812. She and her husband John named the baby Charles John Huffman Dickens, his first name in honor of his maternal grandfather. Elizabeth was 22 at the time, and her father, Charles, had been an instrument-maker before working for the Navy Pay Office, where he was later found guilty of embezzling money and fled England. Elizabeth was known for her energy, her good sense of humor, and her pleasant personality. She was relatively well-educated, even knowing some Latin.

John Dickens, little Charles' father, was the son of a maid, Elizabeth Ball, and a manservant, William Dickens. William, who was already elderly at the time of his marriage, died before his second son John was born. John, instead of becoming a servant like his parents, obtained a position in the Navy Pay Office—a position he could only have acquired with the help of the Crewe family, his mother's employers. Some scholars have even suggested that John Crewe or some other gentleman who visited the Crewe house was John's real father. In any case, what is certainly true is that John grew up watching men who lived luxuriously, gambling and drinking, but also enjoying the company of some of the most revered authors and politicians of the day.

Inspired, John wanted to live the life of a gentlemen of refined tastes. He acquired a significant collection of books—a very expensive investment at the time. He made his way upwards in the Navy Pay Office, becoming assistant clerk in 1807. Since the Crewes were friends with the treasurer of the Navy, John Dickens was well placed for another promotion not many years later. He married Elizabeth, whose brother had been his colleague in the Navy Pay Office, in June 1809. Throughout this time, however, John was also developing habits of extravagant spending and incurrence of debt that would plague his life and later bring disaster to his family.

Charles Dickens and his sister Fanny, two years older, would begin to experience their father's inability to manage money before they were even old enough to remember it. When Charles was just five months old, the Dickens family moved to a smaller house in a poorer area. Toward the end of 1814, the family moved to London for John's work. There, John continued to live above his income and had to resort to asking his mother for funds. Two more children, Alfred and Letitia, were born by 1816, though Alfred died at only six months old. The family then moved again, this time to Kent.

By this time, little Charles was five, and his mother was busy teaching him to read. As he grew, he began to read the many books available to him at home, from *Robinson Crusoe* to the *Arabian Nights*. Charles was sometimes lonely and not as athletic as other boys his age, due partly to severe pains in his sides. He enjoyed performing silly songs for his family and sometimes duets with his older sister Fanny at a nearby tavern whose owner was a friend of John's. The Dickens family also went to the theatre, where the young Charles was introduced to everything from Shakespeare to pantomime. He even wrote his own drama, called *Misnar, the Sultan of India*.

John was still borrowing money at an alarming rate, and in 1821 he had to move his family—now he and Elizabeth had five children, with the births of Harriet and Frederick—to a poorer area once again. This same year, Fanny and Charles began to attend school. The school they went to was run by a Mr. Giles, the son of a minister. Giles had not only studied at Oxford, but he was also a teacher who knew how to encourage and motivate his students. Charles did well at the school, and quickly earned the favor of his teacher. He would later treasure the memories of his life during the period in Kent as one of the best times of his life.

But these days were numbered. In 1822, when Charles was ten, his father's work called the family back to London. The Dickens moved into a narrow, three-story house in Camden Town. By this time, a sixth child, Alfred Lamert, had been born, and they also had a lodger living with them. Charles had a hard time finding friends in this new place, but he did become close to his father's older brother, Thomas. Though John and Elizabeth had money to send Fanny to the Royal Academy of Music when she received a place there, they did not send Charles back to school after they arrived in London. He helped to take care of the younger children and ran errands, all the while amusing himself by writing character sketches of people he met or saw in the city.

Change was coming to the Dickens family once again. In February 1824, John Dickens was finally arrested for his debts. When he could find no help to repay his debts—since he had long exhausted all his sources—he was taken to debtor's prison. Charles, at 12 years old, was left trying to help his family survive by pawning their possessions one by one, from books to furniture. Before long the family was living in two cold, bare rooms.

Help came from their former lodger, James Lamert. He found work for Charles at the factory he managed. Charles, who had dreamed of attending Cambridge, was terribly disappointed at the turn life had taken and at his parents' seeming indifference as his potential went to waste. Nonetheless, he began his new job, where he labeled pots of boot and shoe blacking. When Elizabeth was forced to let the house go and go live at the prison with John, Charles had lodgings close to the prison, where he could see his family sometimes. Even when John managed to get out of prison following the death of his mother, Charles remained at his job in the blacking factory; that was until John had a quarrel with James Lamert. Elizabeth quickly resolved the dispute and got an invitation for Charles to return to his job—an action which Charles would always hold against her. He could never forget this difficult time when he had been forced to work in a low-paying and, in his view, demeaning job as a child, and it would have a significant influence on the stories he would later tell.

However, despite his mother's desire for him to keep working, Charles' life now returned to one more usual for a boy of his social class as John decided to send Charles back to school. He would continue his education at a nearby school, Wellington House Academy. There, he made friends with the other boys and enjoyed playing games, writing a mini-newspaper, and taking part in the school's theatrical performances. A few years later, in 1827, 15-year-old Charles had to put a halt to his education when his father could no longer pay for school. His formal education was now over for good, and Charles once again needed to find work.

Chapter Two

Beginnings as an Author

"The truth and power with which it is made are beyond all praise—so certain, so penetrating, and so deeply-aimed, and yet, at the same time, so obvious and familiar, are the materials employed . . . We place the picture by the side of those of the greatest masters of this style of fiction in our language, and it rises in the comparison. We recognize in this fine writer a maturing excellence."

—John Foster's review of *The Pickwick Papers*

With his mother's help, Dickens acquired a position as a clerk in a law firm called Ellis & Blackmore. He was now ready to begin his life as an adult and a Londoner. Dickens enjoyed dressing his best and making the other clerks at the law firm laugh with his imitations of people, from famous singers and actors to the clients and lawyers of the firm. The following year, he moved to a position with a different solicitor, Charles Molloy. He thought about pursuing his career in law, and though he did not ultimately get far with this, his interest in lawyers and the workings of the law would appear in many of his novels. He was always observant, building up a store of characters and stories. Meanwhile, his family continued to move frequently, though Dickens did not always live with them.

Dickens left his job with Molloy in 1829 and used his knowledge of shorthand to get work in the ecclesiastical courts. With the help of a friend, he obtained a membership to the British Museum's Reading Room and spent his spare time reading there. In 1830, he met Maria Beadnell, a pretty woman two years older than him. He courted Maria and evidently hoped to marry her, but her parents objected to the match because of Charles' family's financial situation. As a result, Dickens sought a better job and soon became a reporter for the *Mirror of Parliament*, reporting on the activity of the House of Commons. Before long, he was also reporting for a second paper.

During this time, Dickens began to believe that the efforts of lawmakers did little real good for the poor and their needs. He would never hold a good opinion of the House of Commons and would later even turn down opportunities to stand for parliament. Despite Dickens' efforts to move up in the world, the Beadnells still did not approve their daughter's connection with him. By 1832, they were actively working to remove Maria from an attachment to Charles. Dickens, never half-hearted in his passions, felt the separation intensely, remembering it later as a time of some of the deepest feeling of his life.

Even through this time of pain and disappointment, Dickens was continuing to pursue another of his loves—the theatre. He attended plays avidly and considered becoming an actor. He even obtained an appointment for a professional audition but missed it when he became ill. Instead, he began to put on a private show in his family's house with the help of friends and family. Though he did not make it his career, theatre would remain a lifelong interest for Dickens, and its influence appears in the theatrical nature of the characters he created and their distinctive voices.

Around this time, Dickens published his first piece of fiction in *The Monthly*. It was a short piece called "A Dinner at Poplar Walk." He published it anonymously and did not receive any payment, yet it was still a milestone for him and an achievement he was proud of. In 1834, he published a second piece. As he began to publish more frequently, by August of that year he felt the confidence to sign a name to his work—not his own, but the pseudonym "Boz," a nickname that he had previously given his youngest brother Augustus.

These sketches were still not a source of income, and the Dickens family continued to suffer monetary struggles. In parliament, the debate centered around the passage of a bill to make amendments to the Poor Law. Dickens likely was present for many of these debates in his work as a reporter, and the ultimate passage of the harsh bill must have made him further question the government. Themes related to this bill and the workhouses that it forced the poor into would appear in books such as *Oliver Twist*.

Through a friend, Dickens found a more secure job working for the *Morning Chronicle*, a growing paper, and he at last had a steady income. But the family troubles increased again when his father was arrested again. Charles, now a grown man, was afraid that he might be arrested as well due to living at the same address. He called on friends and raised funds to have John released. Soon after, John left London in hopes of escaping his creditors. Charles, for his part, felt it was time for him to establish himself as independent from his family, but—always enjoying the presence of other people—he soon asked his younger brother Frederick to live with him.

In 1835, George Hogarth, co-editor for a new evening paper related to the *Chronicle*, took notice of Dickens' work and invited him to publish with the evening paper. This relationship with George Hogarth would also have other ramifications for Charles' life. When he went to visit Hogarth at his home in Kensington, he met the Hogarth family—including Hogarth's 19-year-old daughter Catherine. She was not as beautiful as Maria had been nor as intelligent as Dickens himself, yet, wanting to be married and wary of women who did remind him of Maria, Charles quickly decided to court her. Less than six months later, the two were engaged.

The year 1835 was also significant because Dickens began working on his first book. A successful novelist, Harrison Ainsworth, noticed Boz's sketches and eventually discovered that Charles Dickens was their author. Ainsworth introduced Dickens to his publisher and an illustrator, and work began on the first collection of Dickens' sketches: *Sketches by 'Boz', Illustrative of Every-day Life, and Every-day People* . The collection was published in February of the following year, and through hard work by Dickens and his publisher John Macrone to get the book into the hands of those who would notice it, it received good reviews.

Soon another publishing opportunity materialized for Dickens. William Hall, representing his publishing company Chapman & Hall, asked Dickens to consider writing monthly sketches in a series for 14 pounds a month. Dickens was pleased, as the money would help him move toward marrying Catherine. He had the beginnings of a humorous character in mind already, and this agreement with Hall led to the development of the famous Mr. Pickwick and his adventures. Hall also agreed to publish another piece Dickens had been working on, *The Strange Gentleman*.

Now Dickens began serious preparation for his wedding and marriage, buying furniture and sorting out who was to be his best man. He had asked his publisher John Macrone, who had also become a good friend, but Macrone was married and his wife maintained that the best man should be single, so Dickens had to ask another friend. The wedding took place on April 2, 1836, in St. Luke's Church in Chelsea. It was not a large affair, with only immediate family, John Macrone, and Dickens' best man

Tom Beard in attendance. The couple went to Kent for their honeymoon—the site of many of Charles' happiest memories.

Dickens was kept busy between his reporting and his fiction. He began work on another novel to publish with Macrone. *The Pickwick Papers* also took off, after a somewhat rocky start, when Dickens introduced the character of Pickwick's servant, Sam Weller. The story became widely popular and was enjoyed by readers across all social and economic classes. Soon Dickens was in negotiations with two more publishers, Richard Bentley and Thomas Tegg, as his work became widely recognized.

By the fall, Dickens had agreed to produce so many pieces of writing that the task of completing everything looked impossible. He was also supposed to become the editor of a monthly publication put out by Richard Bentley called *Bentley's Miscellany*. In the face of all these commitments, he resigned from his job at the *Chronicle* and tried to back out of his early and lower-paying agreement with Macrone, causing harm to their friendship. Yet this was not enough, and he was forced to back out of commitments to Tegg and Bentley as well, trying to escape the work that paid the least as his popularity would now allow him to receive more. Dickens started to take an aggrieved perspective toward his publishers, imagining that they were out to take advantage of him.

His last two publications of the year were not on par with his previous work, but at last the dramatic—and overall, successful—year of 1836 ended. The following year was to bring its own challenges for Dickens.

Chapter Three

Increasing Fame

"We enter with him by night, through long double rows of brightly burning lamps, a noisy, bustling, crowded scene, in which he shows us the rags of the squalid ballad-singer fluttering in the same rich light that shows the goldsmith's glittering treasures . . . At all times, and under every aspect, he gives us to feel and see the great city as it really is."

—John Forster's review of *Nicholas Nickleby*

The year 1837 began with the birth of Charles and Catherine's first child on January 5. They did not christen their new baby boy immediately, and in fact, it would be almost a year before this happened—Dickens' intense writing schedule ruled the family. He was still writing *Pickwick* monthly and had also begun work on a new book, *Oliver Twist*. This novel would begin coming out in monthly installments in *Bentley's Miscellany* starting in February. To work on both of these projects at once required significant planning to keep the plots running smoothly. He often barely met his deadlines for the two publications, yet was rewarded for his work as sales continued to increase.

On top of this intense work schedule, Catherine was suffering from depression after the baby's birth, requiring Charles' attention. Charles himself was also experiencing problems with his health. He decided to take the family, along with Catherine's younger sister Mary, out of town for five weeks to return to the place where he and Catherine had celebrated their honeymoon. This allowed Dickens a chance to take long walks in the fresh air of the countryside—though he still had to return to London once a week—and Catherine's condition also seemed to improve. After returning from this excursion, Dickens moved his wife and child into a new, large house—a sign of his increasing success, both economically and socially. Though Charles' brothers and sisters were also finding independent direction in life, John Dickens seemed never to change and came to his oldest son for handouts, sometimes also using Charles' name to get what he wanted.

Though the rest in the countryside and the move to the new house made it appear that life was looking up for Dickens, in May a painful blow fell. Mary Hogarth, Catherine's sister, suddenly fell ill and died in the space of less than a day. Dickens, who had become quite close to Mary, was distraught. He failed to write the installments of *The Pickwick Papers* and *Oliver Twist* that were expected for the end of May and beginning of June—a lapse that would not happen at any other time of his life. Caught up in emotion at the funeral, he even announced that he wanted to be buried alongside his sister-in-law.

He and Catherine dealt with the tragedy by leaving London once again. During this time, a new friend, John Forster, came to visit to try to help and distract Dickens. This became the beginnings of a lifelong friendship—one that would make a great difference in both Dickens' and Forster's lives. Forster became the man to whom Dickens told his deepest thoughts and feelings. The two men were often companions in riding, walking, dining, or attending the theatre. He introduced Dickens to many actors, writers, and artists who became his friends. Beyond this social companionship, Forster supported Dickens' work and advised him, particularly when it came to working with publishers—a matter with which Dickens struggled. Forster helped Dickens regain valuable copyrights—such as that for *Oliver Twist*—which Dickens had earlier sold for a relative pittance, and he also helped Dickens adjust contracts that were made before his rise to popularity. He essentially functioned, for Dickens, much like a literary agent.

Toward the end of 1837, Dickens finished *The Pickwick Papers*. As 1838 began, he made arrangements with Chapman & Hall to begin work on a new story—*Nicholas Nickleby*. This novel would call attention to the terrible conditions at schools for illegitimate children in Yorkshire, and Dickens made a trip to Yorkshire in February of 1838 to do research for the book. He and a friend made inquiries under a cover story of attempting to find a place a friend's son. They could not actually visit the school, but talked to local people—including the headmaster of a school—and heard horrific reports. The first episode of *Nicholas Nickleby* was published at the end of February to an overwhelmingly positive reception. By the end of the year, the story was even being dramatized for theatres.

Dickens continued with his frantic work pace, attempting to finish *Oliver Twist* to be published in book form in the fall. His energy was tremendous, and on top of his writing, he took his family to live by the river, in Twickenham, in the summer of 1838 and to a home by the Thames and later another by the sea in Kent in 1839. He and Catherine had finally named their first son Charley, though Dickens nicknamed him "Snodgering Blee." Catherine gave birth to a second child—a daughter named Mary—in early 1838.

Despite Forster's help, Dickens could not entirely resolve his conflicts with his publishers and particularly became embroiled between Chapman & Hall and Bentley, who were competing for his work. Dickens preferred

Chapman & Hall, who provided better bonuses, and though he could not remove himself from his commitments to Bentley, he sometimes neglected these promises in order to favor projects for Chapman & Hall—such as an idea for a new weekly magazine that would not be a serial but a collection of individual short pieces. Dickens was also disturbed by reports of what was happening with his work in America, where the lack of regulations and copyright laws was allowing publishers to produce his work in any arrangements they wished for their own profit.

As 1839 neared a close, Dickens' third child, another daughter, was born. This likely contributed to his decision that it was time for his family to move to a larger house once again, and he soon located one in Devonshire Terrace. The large house offered more space and an ideal location, and Dickens set about making it his own, adding significant improvements and changes as the family prepared to move in December. Due to this, he once again lapsed in a promise to Bentley and did not produce the manuscript of *Barnaby Rudge*, whose publication Bentley had already been advertising.

As a new year and a new decade began, Dickens finally began to tire from his endless activity, and he hoped to take a break and focus mainly on editing his new weekly magazine. However, this goal would soon prove impossible, and Dickens was plunged back into the business of writing once again.

Chapter Four

The Republic of My Imagination

"Now the coach flung us in a heap on its floor, and now crushed our heads against the roof... Still, the day was beautiful, the air delicious, and we were alone: with no tobacco spittle, or eternal prosy conversation about dollars and politics... to bore us. We really enjoyed it."

—Charles Dickens, in a letter to John Forster

As 1840 began, Dickens' desire for rest soon became complicated by the need to continue earning through his writing and the sudden drop in popularity of his weekly magazine, *Master Humphrey's Clock*. He had hoped to work only as the editor, but when sales of the second issue dropped off dramatically, Dickens realized that he would need to become the sole writer as well—his audience wanted to read more of his own stories, not merely those edited by him. Rather than taking a break, he soon found himself under more pressure, which in turn affected his health.

He began a story that turned into *The Old Curiosity Shop*, a tale of a girl named Nell, all sweetness and innocence, who progresses steadily towards her death despite her attempts to escape. Like *The Pickwick Papers*, *The Old Curiosity Shop* began initially as a few episodes and was not as planned or structured as most of Dickens' novels. Also like *The Pickwick Papers*, this new story quickly achieved impressive popularity and critical acclaim and was soon hailed as one of Dickens' masterpieces. The theme of Nell's death struck a deep chord with Victorian audiences, for whom the experience of a child's death was almost universally personal.

Dickens himself, as he wrote about Nell's death in November and December, worked himself into an emotional state of serious suffering. He refused to even leave home for a short time for fear that something would disturb his emotions, sensing that these feelings were essential to the successful depiction of the dramatic scene. Ironically, even when his good friend Macready's toddler daughter died, Dickens was so focused on his work that he did no more than send a sympathetic note.

The tremendous success of Nell and *The Old Curiosity Shop* carried Dickens through 1840, but the next year he needed to start a new serialized novel to provide material for *Master Humphrey's Clock*. Consequently, he turned back to *Barnaby Rudge*, the story on which he had previously failed to make headway. In June of 1841, as he worked on *Barnaby Rudge*—a story that, in contrast to *The Old Curiosity Shop*, would become one of his least popular works—Dickens also traveled with Catherine to Scotland. There he received a major honor, the Freedom of the City of Edinburgh. After enjoying his acclaim and speaking to enthusiastic crowds, he and Catherine left the city to make a journey through the Highlands. Despite difficult traveling conditions—they once came close to drowning in a flooding river—and bad weather, Dickens continued writing during the journey.

But all was not well. Despite continuing financial pressure, which Dickens' father contributed to by signing bills with a forgery of his son's signature, Charles was desperate for a break. He suffered from several health complaints such as indigestion and felt like he was heading toward burning out as a writer. With Forster's help, he came to an unusual arrangement with Chapman & Hall. The publishers would continue to fund Dickens for a year even while he did no writing, and the following year he would start another novel. Whether or not they were pleased, Chapman & Hall agreed.

Dickens decided to use his year off to travel with Catherine to America, a country he viewed as a realization of the democratic ideals that he held dear. He wanted to see for himself if America was really "the Republic of my imagination," as he termed it to his friend Macready. The Macreadys would take care of the Dickens children while Charles and Catherine were gone. Despite surgery for an anal fistula in October and the tragic and sudden death of Catherine's brother George soon after, Charles and Catherine moved forward with their plans. Dickens finished *Barnaby Rudge* in November, and after Christmas, the couple was ready to depart.

Charles and Catherine left for America on the wooden paddle steamer *Britannia*—a trip that turned dramatic when storms struck and the ship was in danger of being set on fire by the smokestack. When Dickens arrived in Boston, the first city of his trip, he found himself a celebrity. He was impressed with the city, not only meeting academics and authors but also touring factories and institutions such as the prison and the Asylum for the Blind. Soon he and Catherine began to be exhausted by the crowds and the necessity of constantly shaking hands with the hundreds of fans who wanted to meet the famous writer. Additionally, when Dickens tried to bring up the issue of international copyright, the press took a negative view of his efforts and portrayed him as greedy.

Other negatives followed—Dickens was as unimpressed with New York as he had been impressed with Boston. After a huge event, labeled a "Boz Ball," in New

York, he and Catherine declared that they were not going to participate in more public events. He continued to lack support from American writers on the question of copyright, though he did become friends with Washington Irving and meet Edgar Allen Poe in Philadelphia. By the end of February, Dickens found himself disillusioned with America and the way the press had treated him regarding his efforts to work toward copyright laws, and he and Catherine booked their tickets to return to England in June.

The Dickens traveled through Washington, where they turned down an opportunity to dine with President Tyler at the White House. To his disappointment, Charles found the American government no more impressive than the British Parliament. He next traveled to Richmond, Virginia, but was so disturbed by his observations of slavery that he did not stay long. As the spring went on, he and Catherine continued their tour, traveling through Pittsburgh and Cincinnati and by mid-April to St. Louis.

Now began one of the most adventurous legs of the journey, as the couple ventured out to see the prairie and then took a coach along wilderness roads from Cincinnati to Lake Erie. Despite the difficulties of travel, Dickens enjoyed being far from the many boring conversations he had been forced to participate in and especially enjoyed being away from the American habit of spitting chewing tobacco, which he found completely disgusting. Though he was bored and unimpressed by the people he met in Ohio, he did take an interest in the predicament of the Native Americans who were being forced westward.

After traveling to Buffalo by steamship, Charles and Catherine stopped at Niagara Falls for several days in May. The sight amazed Dickens, who found spiritual significance in its beauty. At last, after journeying through Toronto and Montreal and back to New York, the couple boarded the *George Washington*—not a steamer, but a safer, slower sailing ship—to return home on June 7. They reached Liverpool 22 days later and immediately headed to London to be reunited with their children.

Dickens, relying on his characteristic detailed observations and his many letters written to Forster during the trip, began to compose an account of his American travels. This was published as *American Notes for General Circulation* in October—a work which sold much better in America than England, and so did not earn Dickens much money due to the very copyright issues he had tried to discuss. Despite those high sales, the book was ultimately not that popular in reviews—quite a few American newspapers criticized Dickens for what they perceived as his condescending and egotistical view of America. Dickens responded by portraying America and Americans even more negatively in the book he started next, *Martin Chuzzlewit*.

Chapter Five

Ghosts and Growing Troubles

"I shall be ruined past all mortal hope of redemption."

—Charles Dickens, in a letter to John Forster

As Dickens worked on *Martin Chuzzlewit* in 1843, his longstanding concerns about social ills and the conditions endured by the poor continued to grow. He became a friend and advisor to the heiress Angela Burdett-Coutts, who wanted to use her extensive resources to help the poor. On her behalf, Dickens visited Field Lane School in Saffron Hill—one of London's "ragged schools" that were charities purposing to offer education to the city's poorest children. The conditions he found there were terrible, and he made suggestions to Miss Coutts for how she might improve the schools, but he also saw that the problems were so deeply rooted that even Miss Coutts' fortune was not going to be able to change much. He continued to devote a significant amount of energy to working with her and later would help her with developing Urania Cottage, a home for reformed prostitutes.

Unfortunately, Dickens own financial situation had become a problem again. Sales of *Martin Chuzzlewit* dwindled to just a fraction of what *The Old Curiosity Shop* had witnessed, probably due in part to the changing economy but also to the story itself, which was a departure from Dickens' previous work in its attempts not just to portray individuals, but ideas about society. And if the sales were not enough, Dickens would be obligated to pay back a portion of his advance to Chapman & Hall. Dickens became angry because of this and blamed his publishers for taking advantage of him.

Late in the year, however, a new idea came to Dickens—this one inspired by his visit to the "ragged school." In early December, he submitted *A Christmas Carol* to Chapman & Hall. He did the work of designing and editing the novella himself, creating a book that was beautiful but also expensive to produce with its colored illustrations and special paper, which would cut into Dickens' profits. The tale of the stingy Ebenezer Scrooge, his nighttime visits from the Ghosts of Christmases Past, Present, and Future, and Scrooge's ensuing change of heart showcased Dickens' social concerns and especially his desire to depict how selfishness impacts society. The story quickly captured audiences and has remained among Dickens' most popular for over 150 years, undergoing many adaptations. Dickens' depiction of Christmas even helped to popularize the modern idea of a merry celebration that has since taken hold in Western society, as opposed to some of the views of Dickens' day that held that having too much fun was wrong and impious.

Despite the success of *A Christmas Carol*, it did not provide Dickens with nearly the income on which he had been counting. He began to despair that if he could not reduce his expenses, he would be ruined. He soon decided that his only hope lay in removing his family to a less expensive lifestyle on the Continent. But Catherine, having just given birth to their fifth child, was depressed at the prospect. Catherine had been a devoted wife to her often-controlling husband but had never been Charles' equal in energy or intellect (she had hardly had the chance to develop intellectual interests). Though they had seemed to grow closer through the difficulties of their American trip, now their marriage began to fracture. From this point on, Dickens began to indulge in short, passionate infatuations with various young women.

In June of 1844, the Dickens family departed England for the Continent. They made their way to Genoa, Italy, where Dickens found a house for his family near the sea. In the same month, the last episode of *Martin Chuzzlewit* was published, and Dickens, still angry with Chapman & Hall, found a new publisher in Bradbury & Evans. From Genoa, Dickens wrote *Pictures from Italy*, as well as another Christmas book, *The Chimes*. *The Chimes* tried to play on *A Christmas Carol*'s success while making the social themes even more obvious; it sold successfully, but its critical reception was marked by controversy.

In 1845, returning to England, Dickens became engaged with Bradbury & Evans as the editor of their new daily paper, which was designed to promote the more liberal views that Dickens championed. At the same time as Dickens was enthusiastically diving into developing the new newspaper, he also wrote his third Christmas story, *A Cricket on the Hearth*. This tale had less social agenda than *The Chimes* and sold twice as well.

At the *Daily News*, however, Dickens was not enjoying the same success. When the paper entered production in January of 1846, it soon became apparent that Dickens would not work well in the role of an editor of a daily paper. He hated being constrained and lacked the consistent attention to detail that was necessary for the task. In February he resigned, probably to the reliefs of his publishers. While it looked as if the paper might fail, Dickens' friend Forster soon stepped up to be editor, turning the paper's rough beginning around. The *Daily News* would endure for over a half a century more. But for Dickens' part, he was ready to leave England again. This time he took his family—now with the recent addition of a sixth child—to Switzerland. Here, after his two-year hiatus following *Martin Chuzzlewit,* Dickens would begin writing novels once again.

Chapter Six

Personal and Public Hardships

"An author feels as though he were dismissing some portion of himself into the shadowy world, when a crowd of the creatures of his brain are going from him forever."

—Charles Dickens' preface to *David Copperfield*

During the summer of 1846, in Switzerland, Dickens finally began work on his next novel, *Dombey and Son*. He had a difficult time at first with writing in the quiet environment of Lausanne, away from the constant action and activity of London that he found energizing. In a letter to Forster, he even described London as a "magic lantern" that helped him write. Still, the story came together quickly and was published monthly from October of 1846 to April of 1848, when it also came out collected in novel form.

The Dickens family had by this time returned to England once more, where Charles continued his lifelong interest in acting as well as writing. He had been consistently active with his amateur acting group, and now he and friends helped raise money for the purchase of Shakespeare's birthplace by putting on several performances of *The Merry Wives of Windsor*. He was still active in assisting Miss Coutts, and on top of all this, he and Catherine were now expecting their eighth child.

As the year went on, Dickens turned again to writing a Christmas novella. What he produced was *The Haunted*

Man, in which a chemist troubled by painful memories accepts a ghost's offer to remove his memories and allow him to remove those of everyone he meets. The story ultimately connects memory—good and bad—with the human ability to tolerate and forgive others. The development of this theme set the stage for Dickens' next novel, *David Copperfield*.

Dickens seems to have been thinking about his memories around this time; he started work on an autobiography, which he did not finish and later claimed that he destroyed. However, Forster, in his later famous account of Dickens' life, included quotes from autobiographical material by Dickens, which may have been this same document or a similar one. In any case, though Dickens gave up on writing his autobiography, *David Copperfield* has long been recognized for containing many autobiographical elements. Though the narrator, David, tells a story that is certainly not exactly the same as Dickens', many of the emotions that David experiences parallel Dickens' own life. For example, David is forced to go to work at a young age, and though his situation is different from Dickens' childhood work at the blacking factory, the same feeling of being isolated and uncared for emerges. Dickens also, on the suggestion of Forster, tried writing *David Copperfield* as his first novel in first person.

Dickens became quite attached to the novel as he worked on it from 1849-1850, even though its beginning had been difficult for him to compose. He was emotional when he finally reached its conclusion. Though sales and reviews were, at first, not as positive as they had been for *Dombey and Son*, they began to improve once the novel came out in its complete form. The novel would go on to be not just beloved by Dickens himself, but by many. It has since become one of his most famous and well-recognized books.

Dickens was not only working on *David Copperfield* in 1849 and 1850 but had also decided once again to try his idea of having a weekly magazine. Though this had not worked the way he wanted with *Master Humphrey's Clock*, the new magazine, *Household Words*, was much more successful. Other well-known authors of the day, such as Wilkie Collins and Elizabeth Gaskell, contributed pieces that were published in the magazine anonymously. Dickens often organized the issues around a theme and wrote the first and last pieces himself. Dickens paid close attention to editing all the pieces that were included, and he was careful to pay his contributors promptly.

The following year, 1851, was one of personal difficulty for Dickens and his family even though their financial situation was now much more secure. John Dickens, Charles' father, died after a bladder operation. Though the relationship between father and son had often been strained, Dickens had begun to feel closer to his father in the last few years and was quite saddened by his death. In the same year, Charles and Catherine's ninth child, their eight-month-old daughter Dora, became very ill and died. Catherine was away at Malvern with her sister Georgiana at the time, trying a water cure for unknown ailments. Dickens wrote to recall her and warned her of Dora's serious illness, but must have told her of Dora's death in person. Not all personal developments at this time were negative, however—Dickens took a 45-year lease on a mansion in late 1851, and the following year Catherine gave birth to their tenth and last child.

Despite these private affairs, it is Dickens' concern and anger about public affairs that comes out most in his writings of the next few years. England was going through the Crimean War between 1853-1856, which only acerbated his already existing frustration with England's social and political systems. He wrote several satirical essays during this time that were published in *Household Words*. He also wrote his *Child's History of England*, which took a similar tone. But not surprisingly, his fullest expression of his thoughts and opinions came in the form of new novels.

The first of these was *Bleak House*, which Dickens wrote from 1852 to 1853. The novel focused on the inefficiency of the court of Chancery and the misery caused by the problems in this system. While some critics pointed out that the court was already undergoing reform even as Dickens wrote, and therefore his critique was unnecessary, Dickens used the never-ending case of *Jarndyce* v. *Jarndyce* as a backdrop to depict the connectedness of individuals within society. Ultimately, perhaps influenced by his personal difficulties of the time or his disappointment with the state of England, *Bleak House* turned out, appropriately, to be his bleakest and least hopeful novel. This did not hurt its sales or the public's acknowledgment of Dickens' well-established mastery, though not all critics were impressed. The two novels that followed, *Hard Times* (1854) and *Little Dorrit* (1855-1857), similarly have overt social themes related to Dickens' frustration with the government, greed, utilitarianism, and the harsh nature of aspects of Victorian Christianity.

Dickens kept up his almost frenetic pace of life throughout writing these novels, taking part in organizing two plays by Wilkie Collins in 1855 and 1857 (and acting in the latter) and continuing his efforts for Miss Coutts and her Urania Cottage. His relationship with Catherine seems to have grown steadily more strained. When his old love, Maria Beadnell, contacted him, he responded enthusiastically. She had since married and was now Mrs. Henry Winter, and she warned him that she had become overweight and was no longer the attractive girl he had once wanted to marry. Dickens protested that he held the memory of their time together dearly and could still be trusted by Maria now. Yet when the two met, he found himself disappointed by her, and he soon after cruelly used her as a model for an unflattering character in *Little Dorrit*.

He felt that he had spent his life missing out on the companionship that he imagined a woman of his intellectual equal could provide, and his re-acquaintance with Maria only deepened this feeling. Not surprisingly, the trouble in his marriage was soon to become too serious to hide.

Chapter Seven

Rumors and Infidelity

"He does not only read his story, he acts it. Each character . . . is as completely assumed and individualised . . . as though he was personating it in costume on the stage."

—One reviewer's description of Charles Dickens' readings

The divide between Dickens and Catherine, which had quietly been increasing for years, escalated quickly. Though he bought a small house in Kent—the only house he would ever actually own—that he had admired and dreamed of owning as a child, his growing discontent in his marriage cast a shadow over this achievement. In 1857, matters came to a head. Dickens was involved in the production of Wilkie Collins' drama in Manchester and hired a well-known actress, Frances Eleanor Ternan, along with two of her daughters, to play key roles. One of Mrs. Ternan's daughters was 18-year-old Ellen, known as Nelly. Dickens seems to have quickly allowed himself to fall in love with her. He went to visit the family later in the year while traveling with Collins. He simultaneously wrote to Forster about his incompatibility with Catherine, despite acknowledging that she had always been amiable.

Soon he had moved into a separate bedroom from Catherine and even boarded the door between the two rooms. He began to work towards separating from her legally, as well. Rumors about Charles and Nelly were being spread by Catherine's mother and sister. In 1858, he not only forced them to retract their statements but also published a public statement about his private life in papers including *The Times*—a strange move that only fueled the fire of speculation.

The rumors increased further when Catherine's younger sister Georgiana, long a part of the Dickens household, remained to help Dickens while he sent Catherine and one son away to north-west London. Matters were made worse when a letter from Dickens accusing Catherine of not loving her children and of mental instability was published in August—Dickens claimed he had never meant for this letter to become public. He became increasingly angry at Catherine and lost several friendships at this time—including his friendship with Miss Coutts, who angered Dickens by trying to intervene. One of his children recalled later that after Catherine left, Dickens "was like a madman... He did not care a damn what happened to any of us."

Whether this was true or not, he certainly cared about the Ternan family. Their leases in London and later in a cottage in Slough were paid for by a "Mr. Tringham," and scholars have generally accepted that this mysterious figure was, in fact, Charles Dickens. He moved to his house in Kent, Gad's Hill Place, but made frequent visits to see Nelly. Most historians believe that she became his mistress, and there is one record that Nelly may have had a son with Dickens who died at a young age, but other scholars think differently, and ultimately there is little solid evidence remaining as to their relationship.

While his private life became intensely secret—and in fact, in 1860, Dickens would burn much of the correspondence sent to him over his lifetime in a field near Gad's Hill Place, making the work of historians much more difficult—he continued writing novels to great acclaim and also began to engage in popular dramatic public readings of his works. Dickens had already given readings, particularly of *A Christmas Carol* and *The Cricket on the Hearth*, to raise money for charity for various causes. Reading his works also fit into his love of theatre and gave him the chance to enact the characters and voices that he had written himself. He enjoyed the experience as well as the added popularity that came with performing his work. Though he had always valued generosity and also initially found the idea of an author making money through readings to be improper, as time went by, he warmed to the idea. Particularly after buying his house, the financial prospects became difficult to resist.

At last in 1858, Dickens agreed to do a series of weekly paid readings—a choice his friend Forster argued against. Starting in April, Dickens went on tour through major cities, from Edinburgh to Dublin, reading selections from a variety of his novels. His appearances were more like performances than readings—he already had the texts memorized and could adapt them to suit his audiences. Public response was overwhelmingly enthusiastic; it was obvious that despite the controversy over Dickens' private life, his popularity was undiminished. He would follow this success with two more reading tours throughout England, one in 1859 and another during 1861-1862. Negotiations to do a reading tour in America were disrupted by the American Civil War, but he continued to do readings in London and readings for charity as well.

Dickens was also writing during these years. When a conflict with his publishers caused him to want to switch back to working with Chapman & Hall in 1859, he insisted on ending *Household Words*—much to Bradbury & Evan's dismay. He then started a new weekly magazine,*All the Year Round*. This publication was similar to *Household Words* in many ways, such as maintaining the anonymity of authors, but it also had some differences, such as including more serialized fiction. Additionally, Dickens and his subeditor were the sole proprietors.

Dickens used *All the Year Round* to launch his next serialized novel, which would come out between April and November of 1859. This novel would become one of his most famous: *A Tale of Two Cities*. The plot was inspired by Wilkie Collins' drama *The Frozen Deep*, in which Dickens had acted and which he had to some extent helped Collins write. He had long been interested in the French Revolution, having read Thomas Carlyle's *History of the French Revolution* multiple times since he was a young man. He and Carlyle later became friends, and Carlyle sent Dickens, who now was doing most of his writing at Gad's Hill Place, materials from the London Library as he began work on *A Tale of Two Cities*. This novel was different from his previous work in the way the story and characters grew out of events of history, rather than the plot growing from the characters themselves; it is subsequently more action-based than most of Dickens' other works. Some critics, including Forster, were skeptical, but the reading public quickly embraced the story.

When Dickens finished *A Tale of Two Cities*, Wilkie Collins' famous novel *The Woman in White* became the next major serial for *All the Year Round*. During 1860, Dickens sometimes wrote essays for the magazine, but by the end of the year, he was ready to start coming out with another novel of his own. The first episode of *Great Expectations* was published in December, and Dickens continued the story until June of 1861. *Great Expectations* tells the tale of the orphan Pip's development and has been considered by many critics—both in Dickens' day and since—as the pinnacle of Dickens' authorial achievements.

Chapter Eight

Return to America and Last Years

"From the earliest days of my career down to this proud night, I have tried to be true to my calling. I hope that my public believe that I have as a writer, in my soul and conscience, tried to be as true to them as they have to me. From these garish lights I vanish now forevermore, with a heartfelt, grateful, respectful, affectionate farewell."

—Charles Dickens' farewell at his last reading

After completing *Great Expectations* in 1861 and another reading tour in early 1862, Dickens did not start writing another novel for most of the next year. Seemingly depressed, he went to France several times during 1863—some historians think Nelly and her mother may have been living there and that this is when Nelly gave birth to the rumored son who soon died. However, at the very end of the year, Dicken began work on his fourteenth and last complete novel, *Our Mutual Friend*. The writing of this novel came slowly to Dickens, and he felt that he was losing his abilities with age. He may have had less enjoyment in writing the novel than he had with previous works, and as the book was published between May 1864 and December 1865, critics were divided over it—as they remain today, though critical opinion of the work has risen significantly in recent years.

In the midst of writing *Our Mutual Friend* in 1865, he was involved in a railway crash while returning from France with Nelly and her mother. As the train crossed a bridge, it jumped the tracks, and some carriages plunged into the river. Dickens and his companions were not in these carriages, but in one that dangled from the tracks, attached to the car behind it. After being thrown into the lower corner of the car, Dickens climbed out a window to find a key to help Nelly and Mrs. Ternan escape. He then tried to rescue passengers and assist the many injured and dying, equipped with only his top hat full of water and his flask of brandy. When he was at last able to leave the scene, he did not forget his manuscript.

Despite Dickens' calmness during the actual event, his letters hint that the stress took a toll on him afterward. He did stay in touch with some of the people whom he rescued for several years. And the aftermath of the railway incident was not the only toll on his health—while visiting France later in the year, it is likely that he suffered a stroke. Afterward he had trouble with his left foot, and a few years later his left leg, hand, and eye. This did not stop him from undertaking a reading tour in 1866, where he performed 30 readings. As his health declined, he did yet another tour the following year. Though he was often exhausted, he still found that the act of performing before an audience gave him energy.

In 1867, acting against his friend Forster's advice once again, Dickens began making plans to do a reading tour in America. He reached the United States in November, and while he had held on to hopes that Nelly might join him there, the private nature of their relationship and the public nature of Dickens' travels soon proved that this would not work. Dickens did readings most days and primarily traveled on the east coast between Baltimore and Boston. It was winter, the weather was frigid, and Dickens was often ill and sometimes lost his voice. His immense popularity was unchanged, and he found himself less irritated and offended by Americans than he had been on his previous journey years earlier. He even added a postscript to the book he had written after his last trip, *American Notes*, which suggests that both he and the country might have changed in the interim decade and a half.

When he returned to England in 1868, his health seemed better, but his work was, as always, unending. His sub-editor for *All the Year Round* was injured after falling off a horse, and Dickens took on the whole task of running the magazine. On top of this, there were family troubles as one of Dickens' sons became bankrupt and his youngest daughter's husband suffered from cancer.

Dickens decided that he wanted to do one last tour, and he tried out a new idea—he acted out the dramatic and brutal act of Mr. Sikes' murder of Nancy that takes place in *Oliver Twist*. It was shocking and emotional, a sort of depiction that was unprecedented in Dickens' day, and many of his closest friends questioned his wisdom in doing this. But Dickens, obstinate as ever, performed the murder scene in his readings anyway. It was a demanding act and took a serious toll on his health as he went through it over and over. He became exhausted and sometimes dizzy and confused.

It is possible that Dickens' relationship with Nelly had taken a downward turn by this time—though as with everything regarding their relationship, it's difficult to know for certain. Certainly, as he began to plan out another novel, his work took a darker and sadder tone than it had in*Our Mutual Friend*. He planned to produce this new novel, *The Mystery of Edwin Drood*, monthly over the course of a year. He was never to finish this last novel, and though many writers would afterward try to create endings to the mystery, Dickens' own solution is lost.

His health took a turn for the worse in December of 1869. As the new year began, he recovered enough to do several more readings in London, which were intended as farewell readings. He kept up his work on his novel and even remained part of the world of amateur theatre. Yet it was increasingly obvious that he could not keep up this pace of living, the pattern of energy and action that had characterized his life, much longer.

On June 8, 1870, after a day of writing at Gad's Hill Place, Dickens suddenly felt ill. According to the more common version of events, he was with Georgiana, Catherine's sister, though another version proposed by some scholars places him with Nelly. In either case, he suffered a stroke and then died the following day, on June 9. Though he had made other requests regarding his burial place, his body was buried in Westminster Abbey on June 14.

Conclusion

Many critics have pointed out that after Shakespeare, Dickens is likely the best-known of English authors. His lasting popularity has been so great that it has actually added words and terms to the English language. For example, a "Scrooge," the name of the main character of *A Christmas Carol*, is often a term for someone miserly and ungenerous. "Dickensian" can refer to situations reminiscent of Dickens' work in several ways, especially to squalid conditions that reflect the poverty Dickens' stories often depicted.

Dickens' works have left their mark in other ways, as well: now-common ideas about the celebration of Christmas gained popularity through his work, and his depiction of Victorian London has influenced the general perception of the time and place. His works have inspired film adaptations since the days of silent films, and the way he crafted his characters' voices and natural speech patterns was a predecessor for today's world of comedy. Perhaps more importantly, his concerns about poverty and about laws and judicial systems that hurt the poor are a significant part of his legacy—while many specific issues may have changed, readers still find these concerns relevant to society today.

Dickens and his work can be criticized on many counts and always has been. Not all of his novels were great critical successes. When his relationship with Nelly Ternan came to light in 1934, he could no longer be considered a model of Victorian values, and so his reputation as a good man who championed the poor lost some of its power. In more recent times, Dickens' novels have been criticized for their flat depictions of female characters. But, despite the ever-developing portrait of who Charles Dickens was and how we should regard the work he left behind, the importance and influence of his legacy remain apparent in the vast body of scholarly work dedicated to him, along with the film-makers, writers, and other artists who have been inspired by his stories.

CPSIA information can be obtained
at www.ICGtesting.com
Printed in the USA
LVHW080441150422
716233LV00012B/1331